# my wheel of life

## How To Live a
## Happy & Successful Life

by **Roy V. Allen**

Published by RVA MY WHEEL OF LIFE, LLC

For information about ordering *My Wheel of Life*, contact:
royallen@royallenmywheeloflife.com

ISBN: 9798366245531

Library of Congress Control Number: 2022922136

**DISCLAIMER:**

Any decisions regarding health or finance should be made with the
counsel of trained and licensed professionals.

This publication is intended to provide helpful and motivational
material for my children and grandchildren. Some of the ideas,
suggestions and advice in this book may come from other
people's innovative thoughts and ideas gained through more than a
half century of professional work experiences and exposure to
sales training and self-help seminars and conventions. I acknowledge
that all are not original with me.

# DEDICATION

To my children and grandchildren

Ann Marie
Michael
Blair

Melissa
Krista
Rachelle
Joseph
Matthew
Eli
Aidan
Jane
Weston
Tobin

# CONTENTS

# FOREWARD

Over the past five decades while attending seminars, conventions and lectures, I have collected many great ideas and motivational thoughts that have helped me to grow, to improve and to be somewhat successful in all facets of my life.

After much thought and contemplation I have determined that I would like to pass on to other people some of these helpful ideas and suggestions, especially to my children and grandchildren. This book is dedicated to them with the intent that it will help them live a happy, successful, and productive life as they develop good habits and cultivate an inner desire to serve other people.

Some of the ideas in this publication come from other people's innovative thoughts and ideas. I acknowledge that all are not original with me.

# ACKNOWLEDGMENTS

A special thank you to the great people who helped with the preparation of this book.

**Judi Allen**
My wife, for her encouragement, thoughtful ideas & editing skills.

**Lynn D. Davidson**
Creative Director & Project Manager

# MISSION STATEMENT

We stand at a crossroad making choices each minute, each hour, each day. We choose the thoughts we allow ourselves to think, the passions we allow ourselves to feel, the actions we perform and our reactions in response to the actions of others.

Each choice we make is circumscribed by whatever value system we have selected to govern our lives. When we adopt our governing value system, we are, in a very real way, making the most important choice we may ever make. Those who believe in one God, who made all things and governs the world, may make choices differently than those who do not. Those who believe in God and Jesus Christ and worship them through prayer and thanksgiving may make many choices differently than those who do not. Those who believe that mankind is all one family and the most acceptable service to Deity is to do good and provide compassionate service toward their fellowmen, may make life choices differently than those who do not.

The greatest joy we may ever experience in this life is through our selfless service to other people.

The ideas presented in this book may assist you in keeping your Wheel of Life in balance so that you can make responsible choices that will lead you to a happy and successful life.

Ideas adapted from
*The Art of Virtue* by Benjamin Franklin

"When we adopt our governing value system, we are, in a very real way, making the most important choice we may ever make."

# IF IT IS TO BE,
# IT IS UP TO
# **ME**!

# My Wheel of Life

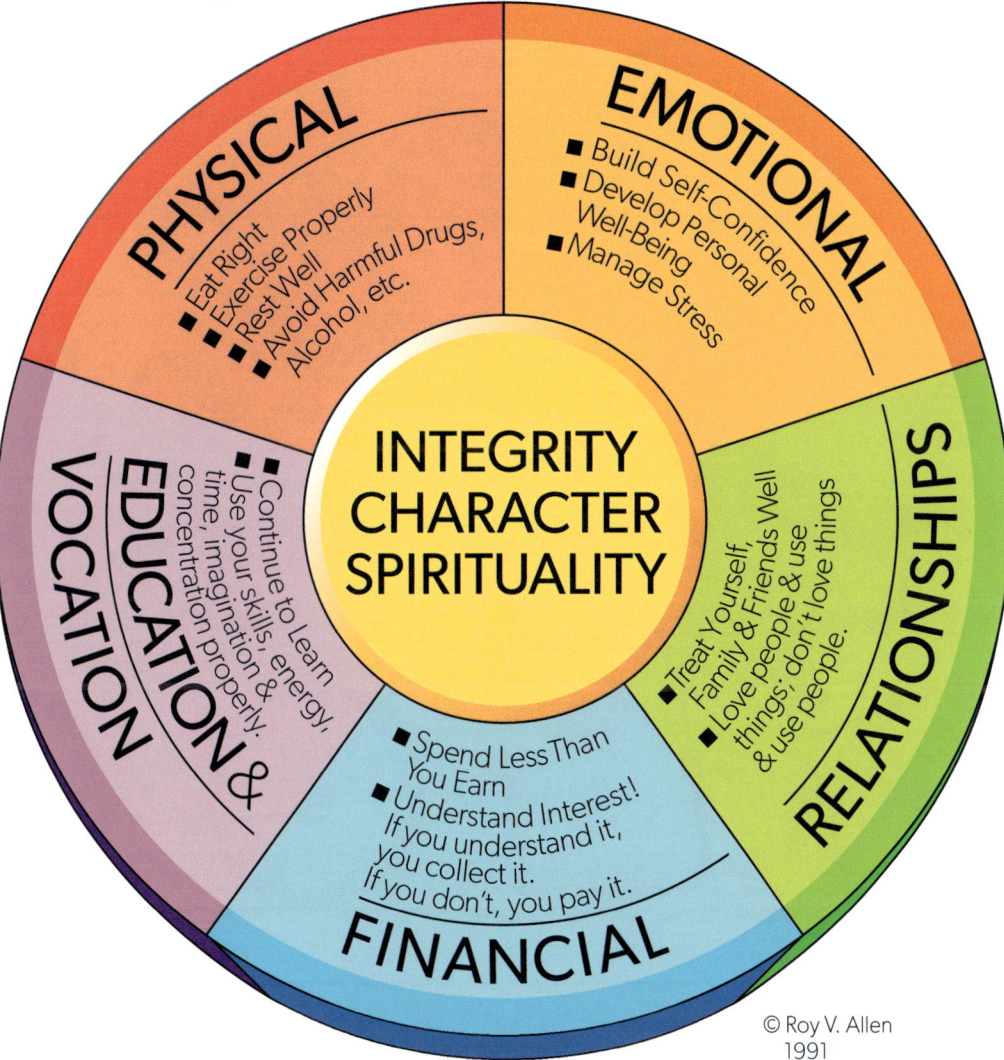

© Roy V. Allen
1991

As we travel through life, it seems so smooth for some and so bumpy for others. Our lives need proper balance in our physical life, our emotional life, our education and vocational life, our financial life, our relationships and our spiritual life. All these areas of our lives are equally important. If we ignore one part of this *Wheel*, will it matter? Yes! If one of these *Spokes* in your *Wheel of Life* is out of balance, it will affect all areas of your life.

Life needs to be in balance to run smoothly, just like a bicycle wheel or an automobile wheel. If our life is out of balance, we will experience a much rougher ride.

My Wheel of Life
**Spoke No. 1**

# EMOTIONAL HEALTH

Emotionally healthy people are able to control their emotions and behavior. They have learned to cope with and manage life's chaotic challenges, build good relationships and lead productive lives.

The emotionally healthy are capable of handling uneven and unexpected bumps on their *Wheel of Life*. They smooth them out and keep moving forward.

Our emotional health needs to be nourished constantly, not just when life presents pesky problems.

Emotional health requires as much of our personal attention as does maintaining proper physical health and wellness. The more time you spend focused on your emotional health the stronger you will become.

Emotional Health encompasses the way you feel about yourself and your ability to manage and control passions and feelings as you deal with life's difficulties.

"Our emotional health needs to be nourished constantly, not just when life presents pesky problems."

## BASIC MENTAL HEALTH ABILITIES

- Ability to get along with others
- Ability to solve problems
- Ability to know what you love
- Ability to entertain yourself
- Ability to take risks

*Good emotional health includes building a healthy self-image.*

## HELPFUL IDEAS IN BUILDING A HEALTHY SELF-IMAGE

- Rid yourself of feelings of guilt. Forgive yourself.
- Forgive others. Rid yourself of grudges.
- Develop and keep lines of communication open with others.
- Give praise.
- Develop goals. Know where you are going.
- Think positively! Use your imagination. Keep in mind how good life will be.
- Compete, don't compare. Compare only to yourself.
- Be YOU! You are unique. Be yourself – your best self.
- Have a sense of contentment.
- Learn to smile. Learn to laugh.
- Have confidence in yourself. Develop high self-esteem.

*"...life is 10% what happens to me and 90% how I react to it."*

*A positive attitude is a real plus in achieving solid emotional health. The following essay was written by Charles Swindoll.*

## ATTITUDE

"The longer I live, the more I realize the impact of attitude on life. Attitude, to me, is more important than facts. It is more important than the past, than education, than money, than circumstance, than failures, than successes, than what other people think, say or do.

It is more important than appearance, giftedness, or skill. It will make or break a company ... church ... a home. The remarkable thing is we have a choice every day regarding the attitude we will embrace for that day. We cannot change our past ... we cannot change the inevitable. The only thing we can do is play on the one string we have, and that is our attitude.

I am convinced that life is 10% what happens to me and 90% how I react to it. And, so it is with you ... we are in charge of our attitudes."

Charles Swindoll

## STRESS AFFECTS EMOTIONAL HEALTH

Stress is always a factor to be considered when dealing with emotional health. Life is hard! We live in stressful times. It is natural to have concerns about faith, family, finances, health, employment and the security of employment.

In order to maintain emotional (and physical) health in today's world we must learn how to cope with and manage stress.

Happy relationships and reverence for a higher power may help to reduce stress.

## HELPFUL WAYS TO MANAGE STRESS AND IMPROVE EMOTIONS

- Physical Exercise
- Deep and Measured Breathing
- Relaxation and Meditation

Regular exercise, regardless of age, is an effective approach to manage emotional stress in your life. If exercise is to be an actual relief from stress, it should not be unpleasant, nor too intense. A brisk 30 to 60 minute walk can be beneficial in setting aside the emotional baggage created by stress.

Even a shorter, slower walk of 10 or 20 minutes can help reduce anxiety and stress.

So, GET UP! MOVE! Then MOVE MORE! Your stress will be less.

## EXERCISE CAN REDUCE STRESS AND IMPROVE EMOTIONAL HEALTH

- Exercise can temporarily take your mind away from worries that cause stress. Take a brisk walk, ride a bicycle, swim laps, mow the lawn.
- Exercise increases stamina and strengthens the body. Even short periods of physical activity can lift the spirit and reduce fatigue.
- When you are physically fit, you will be able to work and play more effectively.
- As you exercise, you have an opportunity to ponder and meditate. Walking or biking provides an excellent opportunity to review goals and to plan and prepare for future events and activities.
- Stress often interferes with sleep. Effective physical exercise can improve emotions and prepare the body for peaceful sleep.
- Becoming physically fit through regular exercise can improve emotions, build sustainable self-confidence and personal self-esteem.
- Self-discipline achieved through consistently scheduled exercise will help to improve your self-image, sharpen your skills and create increased feelings of confidence, personal value and self-worth.
- People who hold to a regularly scheduled, disciplined exercise program most likely have as many worries and frustrations as those who do not, but they seem to handle stressful situations with more ease.
- Exercise will help you develop a more positive attitude on life.

My Wheel of Life
**Spoke No. 2**

# PHYSICAL HEALTH

In this life we have all been given just one physical body. We need to take care of it – treat it well to the best of our ability. Being physically fit improves your chances of living a happy and successful life.

On *My Wheel of Life,* Physical Health is the second *Spoke*. Why? Because the body you have is the only vehicle available to navigate through the challenges of life. If you "mess up" this vehicle, it is impossible to trade it in for a different or newer model. If you fail to take proper care of your physical health, it becomes more difficult to experience all the enjoyable things life has to offer.

Taking care of your physical self can be accomplished by the proper balance of items listed below.

## HOW TO ACHIEVE PHYSICAL FITNESS

- PROPER NUTRITION: Eat healthy foods, especially fruits, vegetables, nuts and grains.
- EXERCISE PROGRAM: Establish a regularly scheduled time and place.
- PROPER REST: A regular routine is best. Go to bed early, the same time each night. Arise early, the same time each morning.
- WEIGHT: It is important to maintain a healthy weight. Step on the scale frequently to check and manage your weight.
- MEDICAL CHECKUPS: Do not neglect routine physical exams with your doctor. Schedule a yearly checkup.
- HARMFUL SUBSTANCES: Keep your body free of harmful drugs, alcohol and tobacco.

BEFORE
SUBSTANCE ABUSE

AFTER
SUBSTANCE ABUSE

"In this life
we have
all been
given
just one
physical
body.

...take care
of it!"

My Wheel of Life
**Spoke No. 3**

# EDUCATION & VOCATION

Prepare yourself with a good education so that you can have an excellent and productive vocation. Remember, work is not work but a pleasure when you enjoy the work you are doing. There is an old saying: *A man who loves his job never has to work a day in his life.*

Be a lifelong learner. The world is constantly changing. New things and new ideas are discovered every day. Make it a practice to learn one new thing every day. Use your skills, energy, time, imagination and power of concentration every day. Make it a habit!

**Successful people do what needs to be done, when it needs to be done, whether they want to or not.**

Be the best person you can be in your work every day. *Give an honest day's work for an honest day's pay.*

Develop within yourself a competitive achievement drive. Set a yearly goal of growth and improvement in your work and earnings. Utilize each hour in a productive manner. Develop new skills. Improve each week.

Be financially motivated, not for the sake of money, but so you can be debt free and earn a comfortable income to support your family.

Be honest! Be honest with yourself. Be honest with your family. Be honest with your customers, your clients, your work associates, your fellowmen.

"...work is not work but a pleasure when you enjoy the work you are doing."

## RULES FOR A PROFITABLE DAY

- Be decisive.
- Act promptly once you have made the decision of what to do.
- Proceed with confidence.
- Focus on the task at hand. Don't get sidetracked.
- Keep your goal constantly before you.
- Start one thing every day.
- Set a standard of accomplishment for each day and keep going until the job is completed.
- DO IT NOW!

"When the sun comes up, you'd better be running!"

## THE GAZELLE AND THE LION

Every morning in Africa a gazelle wakes up.
It knows it must run faster than the fastest lion or it will be killed.

Every morning in Africa a lion wakes up.
It knows it must outrun the slowest gazelle or it will starve to death.

### MORAL:
It does not matter whether you are a lion or a gazelle. When the sun comes up, you'd better be running!

# WHO AM I?

I am your constant companion. I am your greatest helper – or your heaviest burden. I will push you onward or drag you down to failure. I am completely at your command. You might just as well turn over half of your tasks to me, and I will do them quickly and correctly.

I am easily managed. You must merely be firm with me. Show me just exactly how you want something done and after a few lessons I will do it automatically.

I am the servant of all great men, but alas, also of all failures as well. Those who are great I have helped to make great. Those who are failures I have helped to make failures.

I am not a machine, but I work with all the precision of a machine plus the intelligence of man. You may run me for profit or run me for ruin. It makes no difference to me.

Take me, train me, be firm with me and I will put the world at your feet. Be easy with me and I will destroy you.

**Who am I?...**

> "I am your greatest helper – or your heaviest burden."

## ... I am habit!

John Di Lemme

# THE
# WISDOM
# OF
# ABRAHAM
# LINCOLN

## ON
## EDUCATION
## AND
## SELF-RELIANCE

- Education is the most important subject in which we as a people can be engaged.

- You cannot bring about prosperity by discouraging thrift.

- You cannot strengthen the weak by weakening the strong.

- You cannot help the wage earner by pulling down the wage payer.

- You cannot further the brotherhood of man by encouraging class hatred.

- You cannot help the poor by destroying the rich.

- You cannot keep out of trouble by spending more than you earn.

- You cannot build character and courage by taking away man's initiative and independence.

- You cannot help men permanently by doing for them what they could and should do for themselves.

## My Educational & Vocational Experience
# TEACHING ENGLISH IN SHANGHAI, CHINA

A critical component of *Spoke No. 3: Education & Vocation* in *My Wheel of Life* is to have total commitment to an ongoing process of learning in order to expand your educational and vocational opportunities. No matter your age or position in life, it is imperative that you continue to learn new things, improve your mind, sharpen your intellect and aggressively press forward with a well-organized plan and an established set of goals.

## TONGJI UNIVERSITY, SHANGHAI, CHINA

My wife Judi and I are always looking for ways to improve our educational and vocational experiences. Acting upon that inner desire, we took advantage of an opportunity to affiliate with *Brigham Young University David M. Kennedy Center's, China Teachers Program*.

This BYU Program provides opportunity for approximately 80 people each academic year to teach English at various universities in mainland China. Our assignment was to teach English. We were not to discuss politics or religion.

We gathered with fellow China Teachers Program (CTP) candidates at Brigham Young University's campus for two weeks of orientation and training.

In two separate academic years, my wife Judi and I lived in mainland China teaching English to Chinese students at a large university.

Our second academic year of teaching English in China was in the City of Shanghai at Tongji University. Shanghai is one of China's most populous cities (26.32 million in 2019) and a major world-wide economic center. Tongji University is ranked in the top dozen of China's 3500 universities.

We arrived in Shanghai one week prior to the beginning of the academic school year. Upon our arrival we met with the Dean of the English Department at Tongji University to receive our assignments. Tongji's English Department consisted of 167 native Chinese teachers of English and four (4) American teachers from BYU's CTP.

Judi was assigned to teach undergraduate students majoring in English. Her curriculum guide, from which she was to build her lessons, was the ideas she acquired at the training sessions at BYU.

I asked the Dean, Xu Ling, what she wanted me to teach. Smiling, she said, "I want you to teach conversational English to graduate students working toward their PhD. Your classroom is in the Business Building. You will teach 14 hours a week, seven classes, two hours each. Your students have their Master's Degree and must complete an oral English class to receive their PhD.

"In each class you will have approximately 40 students with a variety of degrees: i.e., medicine, dentistry, engineering, architecture, computer science, math and so forth. You will find that most of your students read and understand 80-90 per cent of spoken English conversation. Most of them read English quite well. However, they do not speak English well. Your students have had very little practice in speaking English. These students are very bright. All are working hard to complete their PhD."

So, I asked the Dean, "Do you have a manual?"

"No," she replied.

"Do you have an outline or curriculum?"

"No," she said.

"What do you want me to teach these students?"

She replied, "Can't you just teach them English? Help them learn to speak English."

Wow! A 14-week semester was starting in less than a week, and I had just discovered I was on my own to develop the curriculum from which I was to teach.

After much pondering and some productive discussion on a curriculum with my wife (Judi had been a junior high school English Teacher for several years), I decided I would build my English language lessons around *My Wheel of Life, How to Live a Happy and Successful Life*. I would use the *Spokes* and *Hub* of *My Wheel* as a curriculum outline.

These smart PhD candidates were extremely interested and readily accepted my first few *My Wheel of Life* lessons, but building a meaningful curriculum for 14 weeks, seven two-hour classes per week, was a daunting task.

Each week I worked diligently to create lessons that would fit within or even expand the scope of the *Spokes* and the *Hub* of *My Wheel of Life*.

For example: In a couple of lessons on *Spoke No. 2: Physical Health*, I engaged my students in serious discussions on their personal and physical well-being.

For one of these lessons I organized my class of 40 into 10 student groups, four each, and gave them a blank sheet of paper. I then asked them to draw on that blank page a Ben Franklin "T." I instructed each group to write in English above the top of the "T" the word Smoking. On the left side of the "T" I asked them to write all the reasons they could think of for smoking cigarettes, and on the right side of the "T" reasons for not smoking.

Several students asked why I was teaching a lesson on smoking? My answer, "I am not teaching a lesson on smoking. It is your decision whether or not to smoke cigarettes. You make the choices of how to live your life. I am here to teach you English, and since all of you are very familiar with smoking, I am using it as a teaching tool to help you learn, think and speak in the English language."

Weeks later in lesson discussions on *Spoke No. 4: Finance*, I once again used cigarette smoking as a teaching tool as we examined the high costs of daily living, including the cost of cigarettes. It didn't take long for the PhD candidates to realize that there could be great financial benefits from giving up cigarettes and then investing the money saved to earn interest.

I had them work a problem-solving exercise. "What if I gave up smoking and invested my cigarette money at 4% interest for 10 years? For 25 years? What happens? What happens at 8% interest?"

"Wow! I could be rich," they responded. "Invested money could make me rich." Some students determined that they would also, most likely, live a longer and healthier life as they invested earnings to become rich.

Many students stopped smoking as a result of our *Spoke No. 2: Physical Health* discussions on maintaining a physically fit body. But, it seemed, many more students decided to give up smoking after my lessons on money and investing, *Spoke No. 4: Finance*. These graduate students got excited about investing and earning interest on money saved from making life-changing choices.

As the 14-week semester progressed, I found that many students enjoyed speaking English, especially during class breaks or by hanging around after class. Many said they were trying to put into daily practice the principles outlined in *My Wheel of Life*.

Surprisingly, a large number of these graduate students expressed to me this thought: "American kids are the luckiest students in the world."

When I asked why, their responses were something like this, "I have been in school for more than 18 or 20 years. I have a Master's degree, and this is the first and only class I have ever taken that has taught me how to live, how to be successful, how to have a happy life."

By using *My Wheel of Life* as the foundation for my English curriculum instruction, I am confident that a great many of my nearly 300 students caught the vision and put into practice the concepts they learned in *How to Live a Happy and Successful Life*.

Clockwise: Roy and Xu Ling, Dean of English Department, Tongji University, Shanghai, China.

Roy, Judi, and some of their students at Tongji University, Shanghai, China.

The Bund, Shanghai, China.

My Wheel of Life
**Spoke No. 4**

# FINANCE

*Let me begin this chapter on Spoke No. 4: Finance, by relating a story I used while teaching English language instruction to my PhD students at Tongji University, Shanghai, China. For many decades I have used in my business the Prentice Hall, Inc. published pamphlet, "The Richest Man in Babylon Tells His Secret." I wanted to share the profound principals and financial insights contained in the George S. Clason book, **"The Richest Man in Babylon,"** but my students and I soon discovered that much of the vocabulary in the booklet was too difficult for these English language learners. So, I had to quickly simplify some of the text so my students could comprehend the life lessons and financial concepts in the story while still focusing on learning the English language.*

## THE STORY OF LI
## A VERY RICH MAN IN SHANGHAI, CHINA

The City of Shanghai, China, is an important economic and financial hub in the global economy. This is the story of Li, a poor boy who became a very rich man while living in the City of Shanghai.

Li is very famous in Shanghai and very rich. He gives money to his extended family and to charities and to people in need. Each year Li's wealth increases.

One day, Li's childhood friends, who also grew up very poor, said to the now successful Li, "Li, you are the lucky one; we are not. You have nice clothes. You eat fine foods. Your family enjoys many of life's good things while we are still poor.

"Li, we were all poor while growing up. You didn't seem to be any smarter or work any harder or longer than we did. Tell us your secret. Why are you so lucky?"

Li said, "If you are still poor, you have not learned how to earn money or you are not doing what you learned.

"When I was young, I decided I wanted the good things of life Shanghai had to offer. I wanted a nice home. I wanted to travel, enjoy good food, and have nice clothes. I wanted to be able to help other people. This would make me happy. As you know, my family was very poor so I had to earn my own money. Like most of you, I worked in a factory. And, like you, I didn't earn much money. I thought, I don't earn enough money so I cannot save any money.

"One day, Sun, a rich man, came to me and wanted me to do extra work for him. I agreed and I worked very hard. While I was working for him, Sun told me how to have the good things of life. He said that what he was going to tell me was as true today as it has been for many, many years, even many decades. He said to me that if you do not understand and if you do not do what I tell you to do, you will continue to be poor."

He then said, "Learn this principle: **a part of all I earn is mine to keep**. And so it is with you."

I said to Sun, "Is that it? Is that all?"

He replied, "It has made me rich!"

I asked, "But all I earn now is mine to keep, isn't it?"

He answered, "Don't you pay for clothes, shoes and what you eat? How can you live in a city like Shanghai without spending money? How much did you save last month? Last year? You paid everyone but yourself. You only worked for other people."

Sun asked me, "Li, if you save 10% of what you earn, how much money will you have in 10 years?"

I answered, "As much money as I earn in one year."

Sun then said, "That is half true. Every yuan you save is a worker for you. It earns more yuan and that additional yuan earns even more yuan."

He said to me, "Li, when you understand this, you will become rich. Remember, **a part of all you earn should be yours to keep**. It should not be less than 10% no matter how little money you earn. It can be as much as you can afford to save. **Pay yourself first!** Money, like a tree, grows from a tiny seed. The money you save the first year is the seed from which your tree will grow. The sooner you plant that seed, the sooner your money tree will grow."

I thought about what he said and I decided to do it. Each time I was paid, I took one yuan from each ten yuan that I earned and put it away to save. As strange as it seems, I had as much money as before. Often I was tempted, as my savings grew, to spend it for some good things I would see in stores.

But, I didn't spend it. One year later, Sun came to visit me again.

He asked me, "Li, have you paid yourself first, at least 10%?"

Proudly I said, "Yes, I have."

"That is good! What have you done with it?"

I said, "I gave it to the brick maker to buy some jewels for me in Hong Kong. When he comes back, we will sell the jewels at high prices and divide the earnings."

Sun frowned. "Every fool must learn. Why trust a brick maker to buy jewels? Your savings are gone. You have pulled up the tree you planted by the roots. But plant another one. Try again. **Get advice from people who know about their business.**"

Just as Sun said, my friend the brick maker was fooled, and he bought bits of glass that looked like real jewels. I was sad. But, again I saved 10% of all I earned. I have now formed a habit of saving. It is no longer difficult. One year later Sun came again and asked, "What progress have you made since I last saw you?"

"Each month I paid myself first and gave the savings to Wong, the shield maker, to purchase bronze. Every three months he pays me interest, and I have a feast with wine, fine food and fancy clothes. Someday I will buy a car."

Sun laughed. "Li, you eat and drink the children of your savings that could also work for you. First get an army of yuan, golden slaves, then you can enjoy those things without regret."

I didn't see Sun again for two years. He was now an old man. He asked, "Li, have you become as rich as you dreamed?"

I answered, "Not yet, but I have some money and it is earning more for me. I only take advice from a brick maker about bricks."

Sun replied, "Li you have learned well! **You learned to live on less than you earn.** Next, **you learned to get advice from those who know their business.** And finally, **you have learned how to make the money you have saved work for you.**

"You have taught yourself how to earn money, how to keep it and how to make your money grow. I am now old and my sons think only of spending; they don't think of earning.

"Li, I want you to go to Beijing and look after my lands there and as values increase, I will increase what I pay you for doing this."

So I went to Beijing to work for Sun. And because I have mastered the three laws of successfully handling money, the value of his properties greatly increased, and I became successful and rich. I continue to use the laws of managing money, and I have increased my wealth substantially.

After hearing his story, Li's childhood friends said, "You were lucky that Sun made you manager of his properties."

Li replied, "I was lucky only in the sense that I have learned how to save and manage money. **Opportunity comes to those who are prepared.** I developed the willpower to start again after I lost my savings that first year. I have saved money every month since without missing a month."

Li's friends said, "We are getting older. What can we do to become rich?"

Li replied, "Do what Mr. Sun said. Say it to yourself: **a part of all I earn is mine to keep.** Say it to yourself in the morning, say it again at noon, and say it to yourself every evening. Say it each and every hour until it becomes an ingrained **habit**. Save at least 10%. Save first. Soon you will feel very good and that will help you earn more as you save more. **Learn to make your money work for you.** Make your money's children and its children work for you. Save as much as you can. See that your invested savings earn a good rate of interest, but do not risk too much. Seek the advice of people whose daily work is handling money. Don't try to save too much."

Li's friends thanked him and went away. Some could not understand. Some thought someone so rich should give to his old friends. But a few knew that they had discovered a way to eventually have the good things of life. These few visited Li often to seek his counsel on their saving and investing so that their money would earn a good rate of interest with safety and not be lost.

## RULES OF EARNING AND MANAGING MONEY

- Spend less than you earn.
- Save at least 10% of your income.
- Make money work for you.
- Understand interest.
- Use interest tables for personal financial planning.

# PHILOSOPHY OF SAVINGS

Your savings affect the way you stand, walk, the tone of your voice, your physical well-being and self-confidence. Without savings you are always running. You must take the first job offered, or nearly so. You sit nervously on life's chairs because any small emergency throws you into the hands of others.

Without savings, people must be grateful. Gratitude is a fine thing in its place, but a constant state of gratitude is a horrible place in which to live. People who have savings can walk tall. They may appraise opportunities in a relaxed way and not be rushed by economic necessity.

With savings you could afford to resign from your job if your principles so dictate. Savings give you the ability to provide your most candid judgments to the company which makes you more useful, and therefore more promotable.

People who are always concerned about necessities, such as food and rent, can't afford to think in long-range career terms.

With savings you can afford the wonderful privilege of being generous in family or neighborhood emergencies. Savings shape your personality and character and give you confidence.

The ability to save has nothing to do with the size of income. Many high-income people, who spend it all, are on a treadmill, darting through life like minnows. Take waste out of your spending, and you'll drive the haste out of your life.

Savings represent much more than mere money value. It is proof to the saver that he or she is worth something. Any fool can waste, but it takes something more of a person to save. Waste and extravagance unsettle the mind. Thrift, a form of self-restraint, steadies it.

If you don't need money for college, a home or retirement, then save for self-confidence. A minimum of three-months' income should be readily available at all times. You can't live like a millionaire and be one too. The state of your savings does have a lot to do with how tall you walk.

# INTEREST TABLES FOR PERSONAL FINANCIAL PLANNING

| $10,000 INVESTED | Rate | 5 Years | 10 Years | 15 Years | 20 Years | 25 Years | 30 Years | 35 Years | 40 Years |
|---|---|---|---|---|---|---|---|---|---|
| | 3% | 11,593 | 13,439 | 15,580 | 18,061 | 20,938 | 24,273 | 28,139 | 32,620 |
| | 4% | 12,167 | 14,802 | 18,009 | 21,911 | 26,658 | 32,434 | 39,461 | 48,010 |
| | 5% | 12,763 | 16,289 | 20,789 | 26,533 | 33,864 | 43,219 | 55,160 | 70,400 |
| | 6% | 13,382 | 17,908 | 23,966 | 32,071 | 42,919 | 57,435 | 76,861 | 102,857 |
| | 7% | 14,026 | 19,672 | 27,590 | 38,697 | 54,274 | 76,123 | 106,766 | 149,745 |
| | 8% | 14,693 | 21,589 | 31,722 | 46,610 | 68,485 | 100,627 | 147,853 | 217,245 |
| | 9% | 15,386 | 23,674 | 36,425 | 56,044 | 86,231 | 132,677 | 204,140 | 314,094 |
| | 10% | 16,105 | 25,937 | 41,772 | 67,275 | 108,347 | 174,494 | 281,024 | 452,593 |
| | 11% | 16,851 | 28,394 | 47,846 | 80,623 | 135,155 | 228,923 | 385,749 | 650,009 |
| | 12% | 17,623 | 31,058 | 54,736 | 96,463 | 170,001 | 299,599 | 527,996 | 930,510 |
| | 13% | 18,424 | 33,946 | 62,543 | 115,231 | 212,305 | 391,159 | 720,685 | 1,327,816 |
| | 14% | 19,254 | 37,072 | 71,379 | 137,435 | 264,619 | 509,502 | 981,002 | 1,888,835 |
| | 15% | 20,114 | 40,456 | 81,371 | 163,665 | 329,190 | 662,118 | 1,331,755 | 2,678,635 |

| $100 PER MONTH INVESTED | Rate | 5 Years | 10 Years | 15 Years | 20 Years | 25 Years | 30 Years | 35 Years | 40 Years |
|---|---|---|---|---|---|---|---|---|---|
| | 3% | 6,481 | 14,009 | 22,754 | 32,912 | 44,712 | 58,419 | 74,342 | 92,837 |
| | 4% | 6,652 | 14,774 | 24,691 | 36,800 | 51,584 | 69,636 | 91,678 | 118,590 |
| | 5% | 6,829 | 15,593 | 26,840 | 41,275 | 59,799 | 83,573 | 114,083 | 153,238 |
| | 6% | 7,012 | 16,470 | 29,227 | 46,435 | 69,646 | 100,954 | 143,183 | 200,145 |
| | 7% | 7,201 | 17,409 | 31,881 | 52,397 | 81,480 | 122,709 | 181,156 | 264,012 |
| | 8% | 7,397 | 18,417 | 34,835 | 59,295 | 95,737 | 150,030 | 230,918 | 351,428 |
| | 9% | 7,599 | 19,497 | 38,124 | 67,290 | 112,953 | 184,447 | 296,385 | 471,643 |
| | 10% | 7,808 | 20,655 | 41,792 | 76,570 | 113,789 | 227,933 | 382,828 | 637,678 |
| | 11% | 8,025 | 21,899 | 45,886 | 87,357 | 159,058 | 283,023 | 497,347 | 867,896 |
| | 12% | 8,249 | 23,234 | 50,458 | 99,915 | 189,764 | 352,991 | 649,527 | 1,188,242 |
| | 13% | 8,480 | 24,668 | 55,568 | 114,552 | 227,144 | 442,065 | 852,318 | 1,635,434 |
| | 14% | 8,720 | 26,209 | 61,285 | 131,635 | 272,728 | 555,706 | 1,123,249 | 2,261,518 |
| | 15% | 8,958 | 27,866 | 67,686 | 151,595 | 328,407 | 700,982 | 1,486,064 | 3,140,376 |

| LUMP SUM REQUIRED TO REACH $100,000 | Rate | 5 Years | 10 Years | 15 Years | 20 Years | 25 Years | 30 Years | 35 Years | 40 Years |
|---|---|---|---|---|---|---|---|---|---|
| | 3% | 86,261 | 74,409 | 64,186 | 55,368 | 47,761 | 41,199 | 35,538 | 30,656 |
| | 4% | 82,193 | 67,556 | 55,526 | 45,639 | 37,512 | 30,832 | 25,342 | 20,829 |
| | 5% | 78,353 | 61,391 | 48,102 | 37,689 | 29,530 | 23,138 | 18,129 | 14,205 |
| | 6% | 74,726 | 55,839 | 41,727 | 31,180 | 23,300 | 17,411 | 13,011 | 9,722 |
| | 7% | 71,299 | 50,835 | 36,245 | 25,842 | 18,425 | 13,137 | 9,366 | 6,678 |
| | 8% | 68,058 | 46,319 | 31,524 | 21,455 | 14,602 | 9,938 | 6,763 | 4,603 |
| | 9% | 64,993 | 42,241 | 27,454 | 17,843 | 11,597 | 7,537 | 4,899 | 3,184 |
| | 10% | 62,092 | 38,554 | 23,939 | 14,864 | 9,230 | 5,731 | 3,558 | 2,209 |
| | 11% | 59,345 | 35,218 | 20,900 | 12,403 | 7,361 | 4,368 | 2,592 | 1,538 |
| | 12% | 56,743 | 32,197 | 18,270 | 10,367 | 5,882 | 3,338 | 1,894 | 1,075 |
| | 13% | 54,276 | 29,459 | 15,989 | 8,678 | 4,710 | 2,557 | 1,388 | 753 |
| | 14% | 51,937 | 26,974 | 14,010 | 7,276 | 3,779 | 1,963 | 1,019 | 529 |
| | 15% | 49,718 | 24,718 | 12,289 | 6,110 | 3,038 | 1,510 | 751 | 373 |

| ANNUAL INVESTMENT REQUIRED TO REACH $100,000 | Rate | 5 Years | 10 Years | 15 Years | 20 Years | 25 Years | 30 Years | 35 Years | 40 Years |
|---|---|---|---|---|---|---|---|---|---|
| | 3% | 18,287 | 8,469 | 5,220 | 3,613 | 2,663 | 2,041 | 1,606 | 1,288 |
| | 4% | 17,753 | 8,009 | 4,802 | 3,229 | 2,309 | 1,714 | 1,306 | 1,012 |
| | 5% | 17,236 | 7,572 | 4,414 | 2,880 | 1,995 | 1,433 | 1,054 | 788 |
| | 6% | 16,736 | 7,157 | 4,053 | 2,565 | 1,720 | 1,193 | 847 | 610 |
| | 7% | 16,251 | 6,764 | 3,719 | 2,280 | 1,478 | 989 | 676 | 468 |
| | 8% | 15,783 | 6,392 | 3,410 | 2,023 | 1,267 | 817 | 537 | 357 |
| | 9% | 15,330 | 6,039 | 3,125 | 1,793 | 1,083 | 673 | 425 | 272 |
| | 10% | 14,891 | 5,704 | 2,861 | 1,587 | 924 | 553 | 335 | 205 |
| | 11% | 14,466 | 5,388 | 2,618 | 1,403 | 787 | 453 | 264 | 155 |
| | 12% | 14,054 | 5,088 | 2,395 | 1,239 | 670 | 370 | 207 | 116 |
| | 13% | 13,656 | 4,804 | 2,190 | 1,093 | 569 | 302 | 162 | 87 |
| | 14% | 13,270 | 4,536 | 2,001 | 964 | 482 | 246 | 126 | 65 |
| | 15% | 12,897 | 4,283 | 1,828 | 849 | 409 | 200 | 99 | 49 |

## LEARN THE RULE OF 72

The Rule of 72 is a quick, useful formula that is popularly used to estimate the number of years required to double the invested money at a given annual rate of return. Here is how the Rule of 72 works: You take the number 72 and divide it by the investment's projected annual return. The result is the number of years, approximately, that it will take for your money to double.

# DIVERSIFICATION

In finance, as in life, it's wise to follow this advice: "Don't put all your eggs in one basket."
A diversified investment portfolio reduces risk. If one egg falls, all is not lost.

A diverse portfolio of investments will reduce volatility and yield long-term benefits!

## **2** INVESTMENT STRATEGIES
### EACH CALCULATED OVER A
### 25-YEAR PERIOD

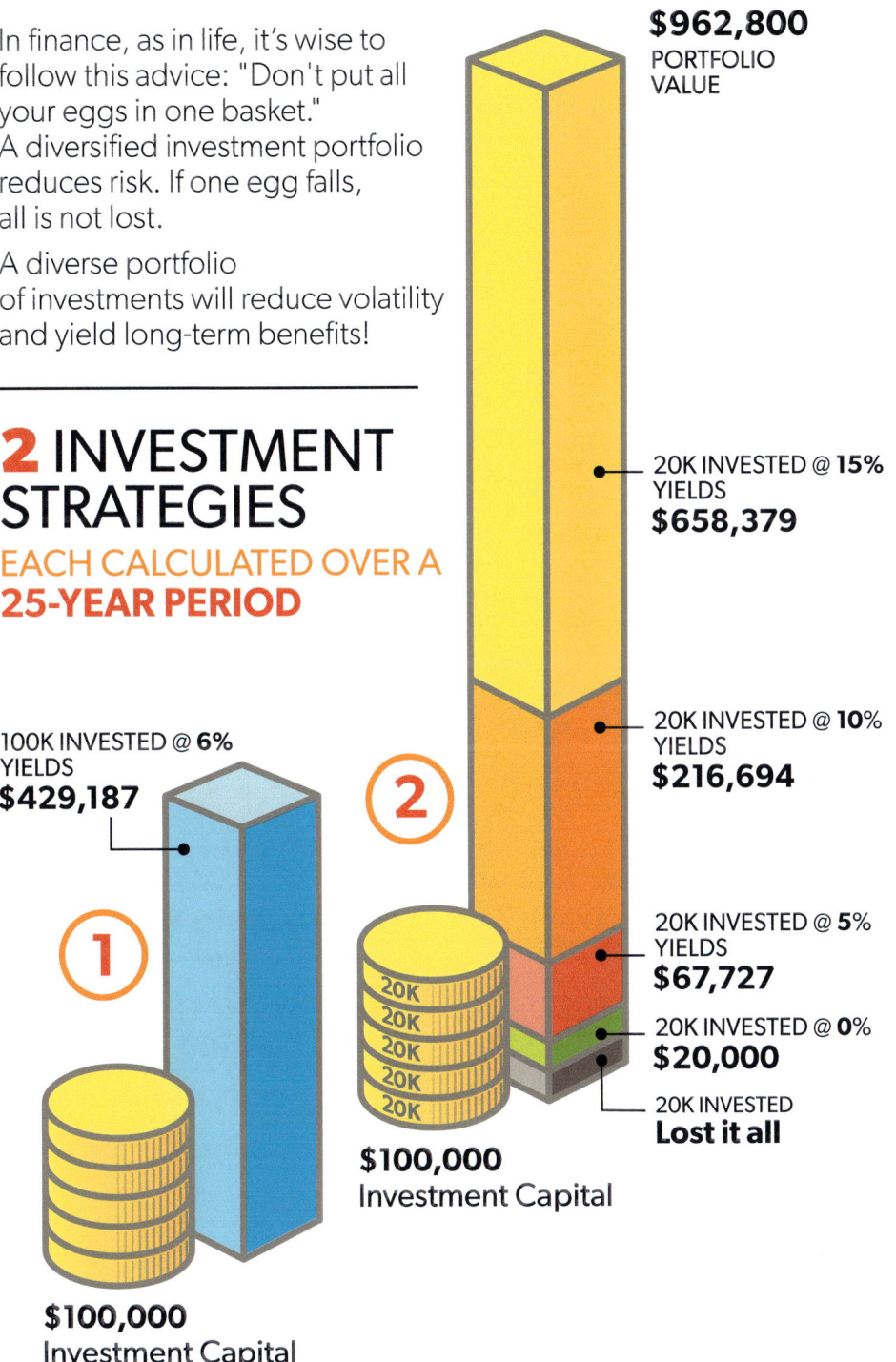

**$962,800**
PORTFOLIO VALUE

20K INVESTED @ **15%** YIELDS
**$658,379**

20K INVESTED @ **10%** YIELDS
**$216,694**

20K INVESTED @ **5%** YIELDS
**$67,727**

20K INVESTED @ **0%**
**$20,000**

20K INVESTED
**Lost it all**

100K INVESTED @ **6%** YIELDS
**$429,187**

**1**

**2**

**$100,000**
Investment Capital

**$100,000**
Investment Capital

## SAVINGS VS. DEBT

One of my favorites:

"Compound interest is the eighth wonder of the world. He who understands it, earns it ... he who doesn't ... pays it."

Albert Einstein

SAVED $10,000

OWES $10,000
[ Charge Cards + Car ]

EARNS 8% INTEREST =
**$800** A YEAR

PAYS 16% INTEREST =
**$1600** A YEAR

$800.00
+ $1600.00
_____
= $2400.00 / yr
$200.00 / mo
difference in assets
between the two households

# RETIREMENT AND FINANCIAL PLANNING

## GOALS AND OBJECTIVES

Have a sense of urgency to do some financial planning and do it now. Approximately 62% of the U.S. population are living paycheck to paycheck. In other words, they have no savings! This doesn't change much in retirement years – less than 10% are living in retirement without financial concerns.

We live in the richest country in the world. Why then do some retired folks have so little in retirement at the end of their working careers? Most people spend first, then save if anything is left. Very few save first, then spend.

## FINANCIAL GOALS

- Saving Plan
- Retirement Plan
- Debt Control - Mortgage
- Children's Education
- Family Income Protection
- Tax Planning
- Estate Planning
- Other

**IF YOU FAIL TO PLAN, YOU PLAN TO FAIL.**

**ONLY TWO THINGS EARN MONEY**
1. People at Work
2. Money at Work

## STAGES OF LIFE

Climbing the steps to financial security is a universal progression for most of us. Our journey requires effort, persistence and planning to not only succeed but to sidestep danger along the way.

**?** When we are living in luxury, do we just keep buying more luxuries or do we keep planning for the future?

| FINANCIAL STAGES OF LIFE | DANGERS THAT RISK OUR STANDARD OF LIVING |
|---|---|
| ■ SURVIVAL<br>Most of us start here. | ■ DEATH |
| ■ COMFORT<br>We're making progress. | ■ DISABILITY |
| | ■ DIVORCE |
| ■ LUXURY<br>We get here with effort and planning. | ■ DUMB DECISIONS |
| | ■ DISASTER |

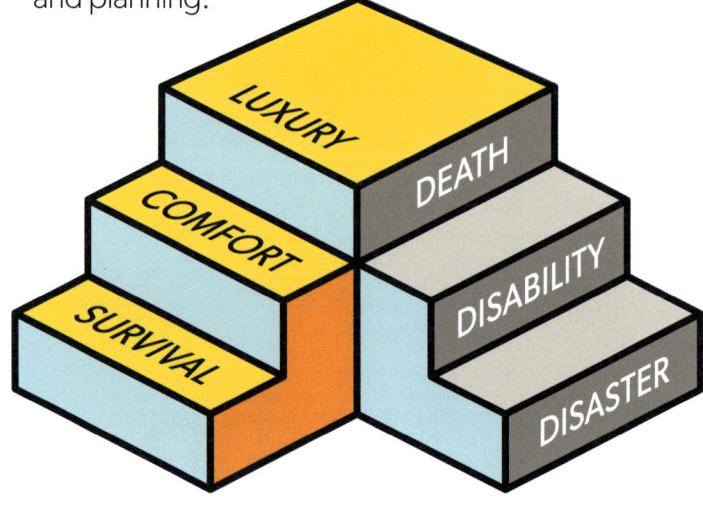

## SIX PLACES TO INVEST

1. Bank
2. Stock Market
3. Real Estate
4. Insurance Company (Life & Annuities)
5. Collectibles ( Gold, Silver, etc.)
6. Invest in Your Own Business

My Wheel of Life
**Spoke No. 5**

# RELATIONSHIPS

## IT IS ALL ABOUT PEOPLE

- **SELF**
  The most important person with whom you need a meaningful relationship is you. If you don't feel good about yourself, who will?

- **SPOUSE**
  Develop and maintain a good relationship with your spouse. You need to work on it daily. Keep the courtship going.

- **CHILDREN**
  Each child is important. Work on keeping those relationships in excellent condition. Insure that lines of communication are always open.

- **EXTENDED FAMILY**

- **FRIENDS & ASSOCIATES**

"The most important person with whom you need a meaningful relationship is **you**."

# THE ART OF GETTING ALONG

Sooner or later, a man or woman, if they are wise, discover that life is a mixture of good days and bad, victory and defeat, give and take. They learn that it doesn't pay to be an over-sensitive soul; that they should let some things go, pass by, like water off a duck's back. They learn that those who lose their temper usually lose out. They learn all people, now and then, have burnt toast for breakfast, and that they should not take another person's grouchiness too seriously. They learn that carrying a chip on their shoulder is the easiest way to end up in a fight. They learn the quickest way to become unpopular is to carry tales and gossip about others. They learn that buck-passing always turns out to be a boomerang – that it never pays.

They come to realize that the business could run along perfectly well without them. They learn that it does not matter so much who gets the credit so long as the business shows a profit. They learn that even the janitor is human and that it doesn't do any harm to smile and say, "Good morning," even if it is raining. They learn that most of the other employees are as ambitious as they are, they have brains that are as good or better, and that hard work and not cleverness or luck is the secret of success. They learn to sympathize with the youngster coming into the business because they remember how bewildered they were when they first started. They learn not to worry when they lose an order or a sale because experience has shown that if they always give their best, their average will break pretty well.

They learn that no one person ever got to first base alone, and that it is only through cooperative effort that we move on to better things. They learn that bosses are not monsters, trying to squeeze the last ounce of work out of them for the least amount of pay, but that bosses are usually fine people who have succeeded through hard work and who want to do the right thing. They learn that folks are not any harder to get along with in one place than another, and that "getting along" depends about ninety-eight percent on their own behavior.

Wilferd A. Peterson

# Lessons from Geese

**FACT 1:** As each goose flaps its wings, it creates an "uplift" for the bird that follows. By flying in a "V" formation, the whole flock adds 71% greater flying range than if each bird flew alone.

**LESSON:** *People who share a common direction and sense of community can get where they are going quicker and easier because they are traveling on the thrust of one another.*

**FACT 2:** When a goose falls out of formation, it suddenly feels the drag and resistance of flying alone. It quickly moves back into formation to take advantage of the lifting power of the bird immediately in front of it.

**LESSON:** *If we have as much sense as a goose, we stay in formation with those headed where we want to go. We are willing to accept their help and give our help to others.*

**FACT 3:** When the lead goose tires, it rotates back into the formation, and another goose flies to the point position.

**LESSON:** *It pays to take turns doing the hard tasks and sharing leadership. As with geese, people are interdependent on each other's skills, capabilities and unique arrangements of gifts, talents and resources.*

**FACT 4:** The geese flying in formation honk to encourage those in front to keep up their speed.

**LESSON:** *We need to make sure our honking is encouraging. In groups where there is encouragement, production is greater. The power of encouragement [to stand by one's heart or core values and encourage the heart and core of others] is the quality of honking we seek.*

**FACT 5:** When a goose gets sick, wounded or shot down, two geese drop out of formation and follow it down to help or protect it. They stay with it until it dies or is able to fly again. Then they launch out with another formation or catch up with the flock.

**LESSON:** *If we have as much sense as geese, we will stand by each other in difficult times as well as when we are strong.*

## ACCOUNTABILITY

# BALANCED BEHAVIOR

I am accountable for what happens to me in life.

When I want to change something in my life or accomplish something significant, I make myself a promise of what I am going to do, and then I keep that promise!

# UNBALANCED BEHAVIOR

I rationalize, justify, blame and excuse.

If I am unprepared to assume accountability for my life, then I must be prepared to be led by someone else, in their direction, at their speed, toward their goals.

"I use not only all the brains I have, but all I can borrow."

Woodrow Wilson

## THE
# RATTLESNAKE

"We can decide to forgive in advance."

A man is bitten by a rattlesnake. He must quickly make a choice: should he chase down the snake and kill it to avenge the offense, or should he immediately tend to his wound? If he kills the snake, he will get his revenge on the creature that has caused him pain. However, this rash act would neither dull the pain nor delay the onset of the poison. If he chooses instead to address the problem and tend to the wound, he will not have his revenge – but he may save his life in the process. Choosing this course of action ahead of time helps him take lifesaving steps as quickly as possible and avoid prolonged suffering.

We can apply the same pattern when others hurt us with their remarks or actions. We can decide to forgive in advance. While it is not likely that a rattlesnake will bite us, it is likely that we will be on the receiving end of intentional or unintentional negative remarks or actions from others in our lives. Anticipating that and forgiving ahead of time keeps the "poison" out of our system and spares us from unnecessary pain and suffering.

## FUNDAMENTALS FOR SUCCESS IN DEALING WITH PEOPLE

"Seek to learn from the ideas and feelings of others."

- Remember their name. The sweetest and most important sound to a person is their name.
- Avoid arguments.
- Be friendly.
- Be kind.
- Be fair.
- Be honest.
- Listen to understand.
- Seek to learn from the ideas and feelings of others.
- If you make a mistake, quickly own up to it.
- Respect the other person's dignity. Value their point of view.
- Be genuinely interested in people you talk with. Encourage them to talk about themselves, their interests.
- Help others to feel important.
- Acknowledge others' good ideas.
- Ask questions rather than making statements that may be somewhat controversial.
- Allow others to save face.
- Praise any and every growth and improvement.
- Give sincere and honest appreciation.
- Always greet people in a friendly way.
- Know when to talk.
- Know when not to talk and when to listen.

## BE POSITIVE!

- Say something positive to every person you meet.
- See something positive everyday in every situation.
- Always think "it might work."
- Practice positive expectations.
- Discipline yourself to become a positive reactionary.

My Wheel of Life
**THE HUB**

# INTEGRITY CHARACTER SPIRITUALITY

At the core of any functioning wheel is the hub. The hub is the strength of the wheel. It keeps the spokes aligned, making it possible for the wheel to rotate and move forward.

The *Hub* of *My Wheel of Life* is the personal traits of *INTEGRITY, CHARACTER AND SPIRITUALITY*. Each are vital to living a successful and happy life.

## INTEGRITY
- Be honest with people.
- Be fair with people. A clear conscience is the softest pillow you will ever lay your head on.
- Give service to others. The greatest joy you will get out of life is helping other people.
- Help others to grow and develop.
- Be patient.
- Keep your *Wheel of Life* round and in balance so that as you live a happy and successful life, you will have the ability to help people you meet along the way.

## CHARACTER
**If it is not true, don't say it.**
**If it is not yours, don't take it.**
**If it is not right, don't do it.**

## SPIRITUALITY
- Know who you are.
- Know where you came from -- why you are here – where you are going.
- Remember, you are accountable for what happens to you in life.
- Make prayer and meditation a part of your life as you seek to find your place in the universe.

## LOVE

Love kindles joy in the human heart. Love greatly enriches both giver and receiver. Love is the only thing in the world which a person cannot give or get too much of. Love – something we all yearn for – is vital to the soul.

A physician once said, "I have been practicing medicine for more than thirty years, and I have written many prescriptions trying to cure ills, but I have learned that for most of what ails the human spirit, the best medicine is love."

Someone asked the physician, "What happens if it doesn't work?"

"Double the dosage," the doctor replied.

Most marriages, as well as other love relationships, are capable of blossoming if we are willing to cultivate them. So that love in our relationships does not wither or wane, we need to act as gardeners, giving the relationship the nutrients and minerals necessary to develop strong roots. If we are willing to carefully water, weed, and cultivate our relationships, ultimately we too can have beautiful flowers.

To love is to give without thought or expectation of receiving. Love considers the safety, growth, happiness and well-being of another. Love offers quiet understanding, loyalty and forgiveness.

> "Love considers the safety, growth, happiness and well-being of another."

**EVERY PERSON
NEEDS THREE THINGS
IN LIFE**

**1**

**SOMEONE
TO LOVE!**

**2**

**SOMETHING
TO DO!**

**3**

**SOMETHING
TO LOOK
FORWARD TO!**

## HAPPINESS

An important character trait is to be a happy person, to smile and to laugh. To laugh is to love, to laugh is to understand, to laugh is to forgive. Laughter can bring a feeling of ease with people who are not normally at ease with themselves or others.

A smile costs nothing, but it creates much. A smile enriches happiness in the home, fosters goodwill in business and is the countersign of friends. A smile is rest to the weary, daylight to the discouraged, sunshine to the sad and nature's best antidote for trouble.

A smile cannot be begged, bought, borrowed or stolen. It is no earthly good to anyone until it is given away. So, if in the course of the day some of your friends or neighbors are too tired to give a smile, why don't you give them one of yours. For nobody needs a smile as much as those who have none to give.

Dale Carnegie

"A smile enriches happiness in the home, fosters goodwill in business and is the countersign of friends."

# LIVING A HAPPY LIFE

## Have a Positive Attitude
- Have self-confidence.
- Know that you are important.
- Believe that you are a good person.
- Know that you can and will do well.

## Keep Your Body Healthy
- Eat only healthy food, especially fruits and vegetables.
- Exercise regularly.
- Have proper rest.
- Avoid harmful drugs.
- Avoid alcohol and tobacco.

## Prepare for a Good Occupation and Vocation
- Get a good education.
- Be a lifelong learner.
- Use your skills, energy, time, imagination and concentration every day.
- Be the best person you can in your work.

## Learn the Three Rules of Managing Money
- Spend less than you earn.
- Get and take advice about money from those who know their business.
- Make money work for you. Understand interest.

## Have Good Relationships
- With yourself.
- With your spouse and family.
- With your extended family.
- With friends and associates.

## Feel Good Inside
- Be honest with people.
- Be fair with people.
- Be patient with people.
- Give service to people.
- Help other people to grow and develop.
- Learn to laugh and to smile.

**The greatest joy that you will get in life is helping other people. Prepare yourself so that you can.**

# ASK YOURSELF:

Is it possible to grow and improve all *Spokes* and the *Hub* of my personal *Wheel of Life* so that I can be more comfortable in helping other people? The answer is YES! Remember, the greatest joy you will get out of life is helping other people.

**When your personal *My Wheel of Life* is balanced with growing goals, you are living a happy, successful and productive life.**

# CHECK LIST
## FOR *MY WHEEL OF LIFE*

☐ **Spoke No. 1: Emotional Health**
Are you able to control your attitude, sadness, anger, happiness, etc.? What areas of your life do you need to work on to be comfortable?

☐ **Spoke No. 2: Physical Health**
If it's too warm, we want to be cooler. If it's too cold, we want to get to a place where it's warmer. These same principles apply to eating, exercise and physical fitness. Are you comfortable with your weight, physical fitness and general well-being?

☐ **Spoke No. 3: Education & Vocation**
If you are not comfortable with your level of education, what do you do? You make a decision to improve your education, and then map out a plan of action to make it happen.

☐ **Spoke No. 4: Finance**
Are you comfortable with your earnings and investments? If not, do you have a plan to make the changes that will bring you more comfort? How? When?

☐ **Spoke No. 5: Relationships**
Are all of your personal and business relationships comfortable? Are you comfortable with yourself, your spouse, family, neighbors, clients and customers? What must you do to move all your relationships to a higher level of comfort?

☐ **The Hub: Integrity, Character, Spirituality**
The *Hub* of your *Wheel* holds all the other parts of your life together. If the *Hub* of your *Wheel* is strong and steady, well greased with love, kindness and honor, you will be living a happy life. As the *Hub* of your *Wheel of Life* grows, improves in strength, vigor and vitality, the *Spokes* in your *Wheel* will likewise improve and grow.

The most basic need of every human being is to be comfortable.

# ADAPTING
## *MY WHEEL OF LIFE* TO YOUR LIFE

Over the years I have presented *My Wheel of Life* to large business conventions and seminars, to smaller groups and to hundreds of individuals. The reception at these presentations has always been a resounding success.

Several businessmen have reported back to me that they have taken the concept of *My Wheel of Life* and adapted it to their particular vocation and work experiences. They developed for themselves a separate *Wheel* focused entirely on *Spoke No. 4: Education & Vocation*.

I encourage you to do the same. Develop a separate *Wheel* for any one of the *Spokes*.

Following are two examples of adapting and expanding the *Wheel* concept to help keep your life in balance.

**EXAMPLE NUMBER ONE:**
An Agent for an Insurance Company

# MY WORK
# WHEEL OF SUCCESS

Because I am committed to be a successful, long-term agent, I must keep my Wheel of Success balanced with these characteristics.

## INTELLIGENCE & LEARNING

- I learn, know and use sales tracks that are either produced or approved by my company.
- I am familiar with and understand the products sold by my company and am very capable of fitting these products to clients' needs and situations.
- I have a commitment to continue to learn about new products, ideas and sales methods.

## COMPETITIVE & ACHIEVEMENT DRIVE

- I have a strong desire to achieve all I can and to be the very best in my areas of work.
- I am very competitive and each year will do better in sales, service and earnings than the year before.

## INTEGRITY & CHARACTER

- I am honest in my dealings with myself, my clients and prospective clients, my family and my fellowmen.
- I am loyal to my company.
- If business can be written, it will be written with my company.
- I treat my clients as they would treat themselves in a similar situation.

## FINANCIALLY MOTIVATED

- I want and provide an above average living for myself and my family.
- I manage my finances well and stay out of debt.
- My family enjoys a nice home, good food and clothes, and they attend schools of their own choosing.
- I have adequate life insurance, retirement, disability income insurance and have at least three months' income in reserve for emergencies.

## HIGH ENERGY LEVEL

- I put in a full day's work each day.
- I am very energetic.
- I utilize each and every hour in a productive manner: making appointments, preparing illustrations, going on appointments and developing the skills to be a master prospector.

**EXAMPLE NUMBER TWO:**
An Executive for a Credit Reporting Company

# HORIZON CREDIT SERVICES WHEEL OF SUCCESS

Because I am committed to be a successful Account Executive, I must keep my Wheel of Success balanced with these characteristics.

## INTELLIGENCE & LEARNING

- I am familiar with and understand all the products and services offered by our company.
- I have a commitment to continue to learn about new products, new ideas and new sales methods in our ever-changing industry.

## ACHIEVEMENT & COMPETITIVE DRIVE

- I have a strong desire to achieve all my goals and to be the very best in my areas of work.
- I am self-motivated and a self-starter.
- I am very competitive and each year will do better in sales, service and earnings than the year before.

## INTEGRITY & CHARACTER

- I am honest in my dealings with myself, my clients, prospective clients and my family.
- I am loyal to Horizon Credit Services.
- I treat my clients as they would treat themselves in a similar situation.

## FINANCIALLY MOTIVATED

- I want to provide an above average living for myself and my family.
- I will use my sales and marketing experience to reach my professional goals and receive financial gain.

## HIGH ENERGY LEVEL

- I put in a full day's work each work day.
- I am very energetic and passionate.
- I utilize each and every hour in a productive manner, making appointments, cold calling, going on appointments, training clients and further developing my skills in sales.

Creating a separate *Wheel* for any one of the *Spokes* of *My Wheel of Life* may help you keep your own *Wheel of Life* in balance.

# IF IT IS TO BE, IT IS UP TO ME!

My Wheel of Life
**WORKSHEET**

## MY GOALS · 20........:

MY NO.1 EMOTIONAL GOAL:

MY NO.1 PHYSICAL GOAL:

MY NO.1 EDUCATIONAL GOAL:

MY NO.1 VOCATIONAL GOAL:

MY NO.1 FINANCIAL GOAL:

MY NO.1 RELATIONSHIP GOAL:

MY NO.1 SPIRITUAL GOAL:

IF IT IS TO BE,

IT IS UP TO

**ME!**

Made in United States
Troutdale, OR
01/07/2025

27737831R00033